2009 GREATEST Pop & MOVIE Hits

Arranged by Carol Matz

THE BIGGEST MOVIES ★ THE GREATEST ARTISTS

CONTENTS

D1597070

2009

Alfred Music Publishing Co., Inc.
P.O. Box 10003
Van Nuys, CA 91410-0003
alfred.com

Copyright © MMIX by Alfred Music Publishing Co., Inc.
All rights reserved. Printed in USA.

ISBN-10: 0-7390-6269-7
ISBN-13: 978-0-7390-6269-2

1, 2, 3, 4

Words and Music by Tom Higgenson
Arranged by Carol Matz

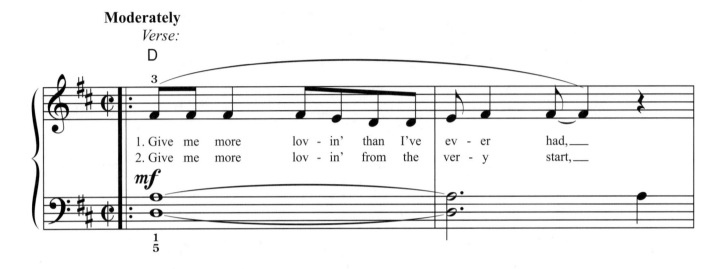

Moderately
Verse:

1. Give me more lov - in' than I've ev - er had,___
2. Give me more lov - in' from the ver - y start,___

make it all bet - ter when I'm feel - ing sad,___ tell me that I'm spe - cial e - ven
piece me back to - geth - er when I fall a - part,___ tell me things you nev - er e - ven

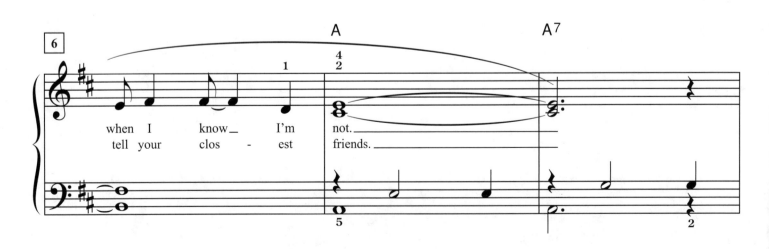

when I know___ I'm not.___
tell your clos - est friends.___

Make it feel good when it hurts so bad,___ bare - ly get mad.
Make it feel good when it hurts so bad,___ best that I've had.

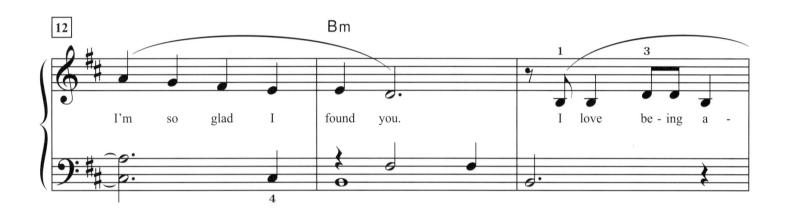

I'm so glad I found you. I love be - ing a -

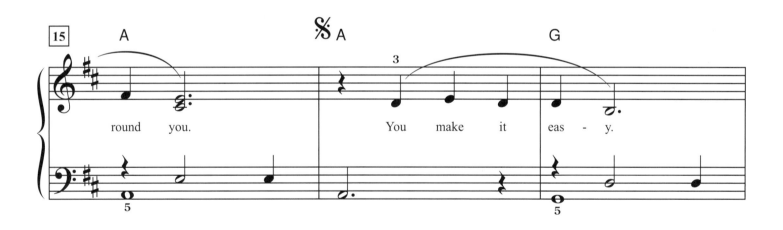

round you. You make it eas - y.

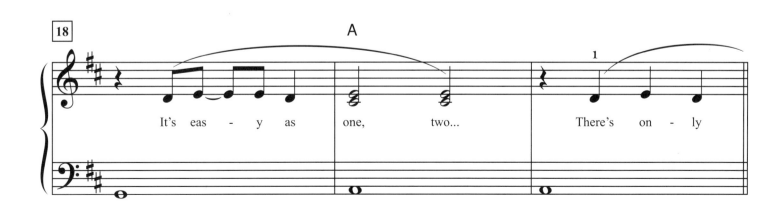

It's eas - y as one, two... There's on - ly

Chorus:

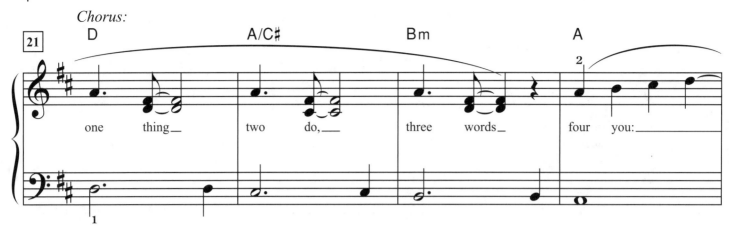

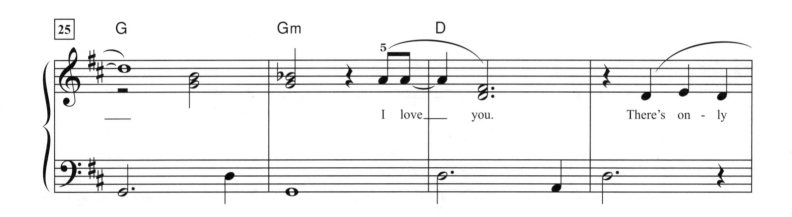

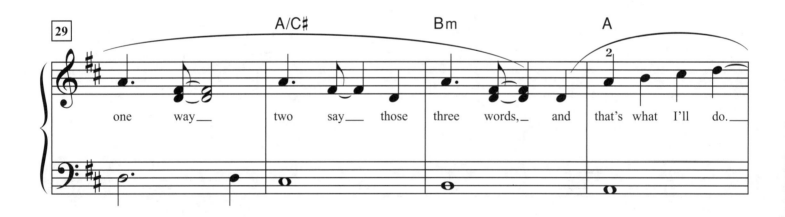

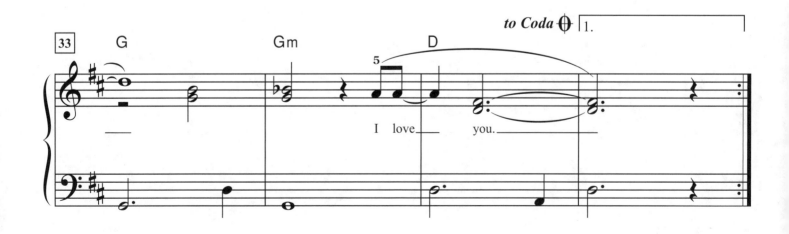

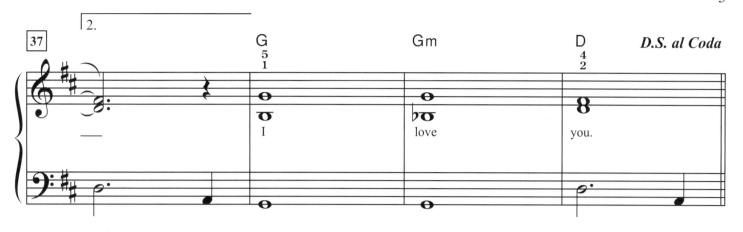

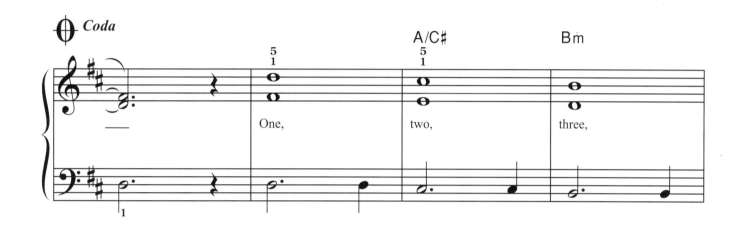

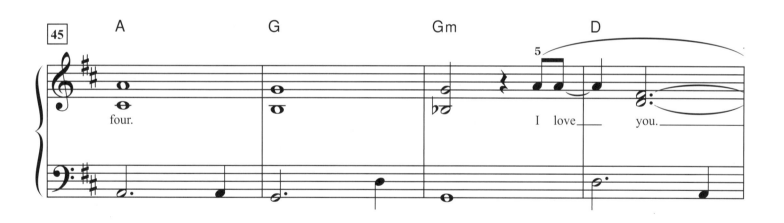

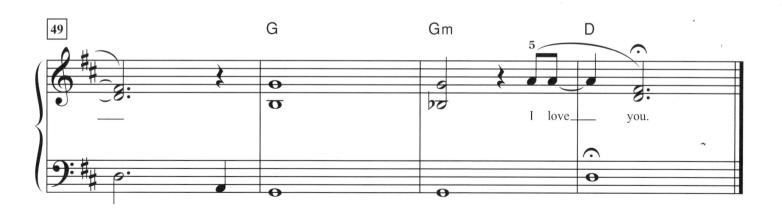

AT LAST

(from *Cadillac Records*)

Music by Harry Warren
Lyrics by Mack Gordon
Arranged by Carol Matz

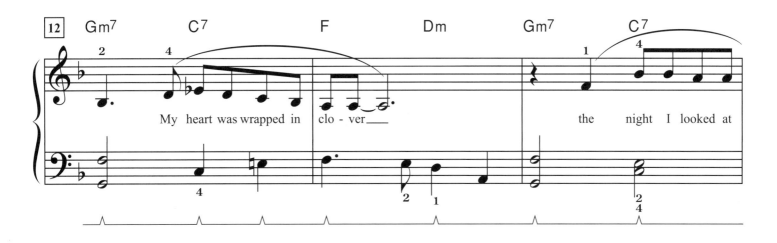

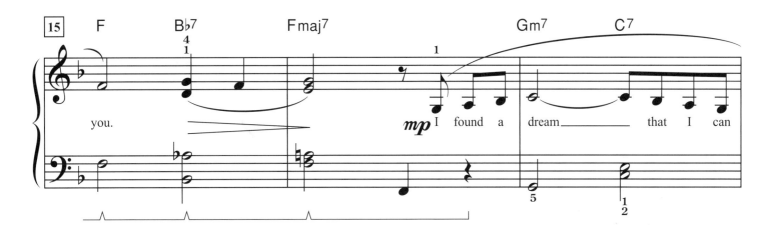

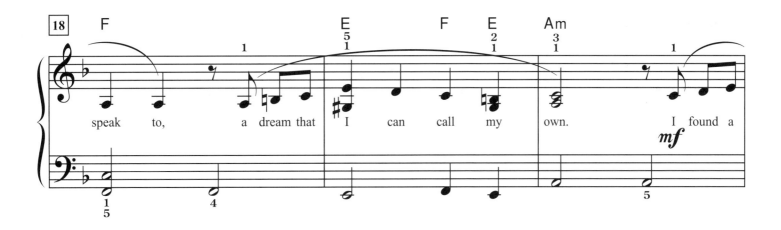

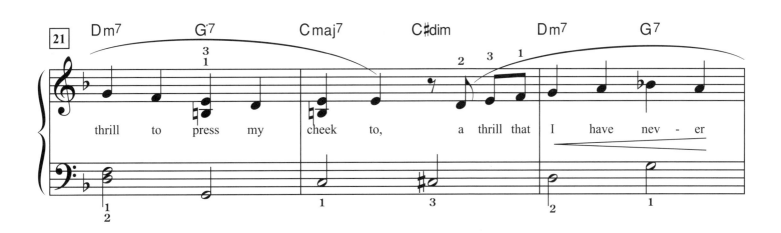

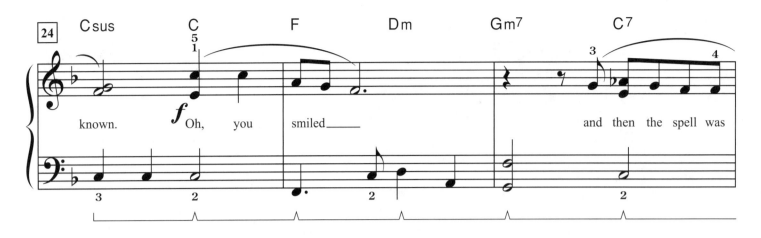

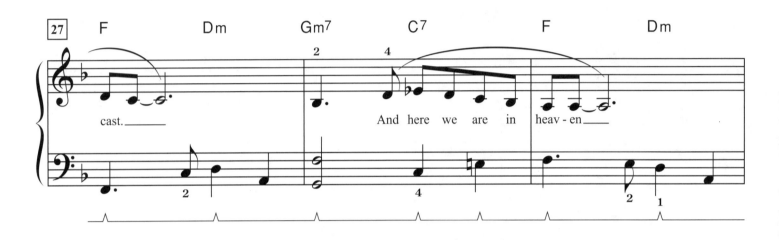

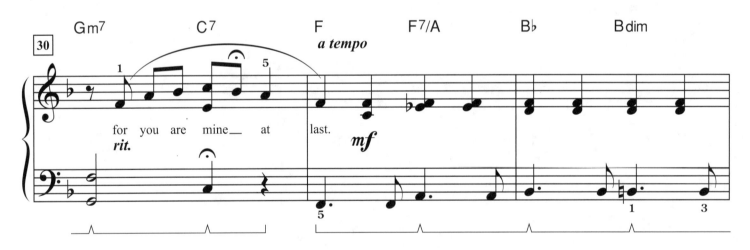

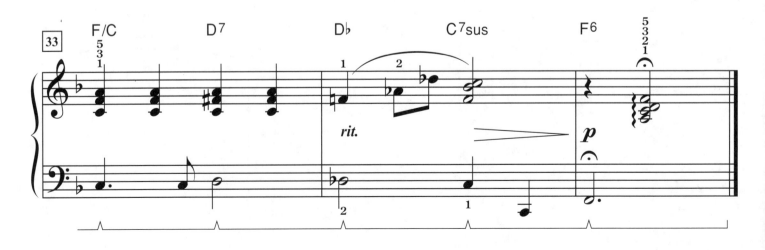

BAD

Written and Composed by Michael Jackson
Arranged by Carol Matz

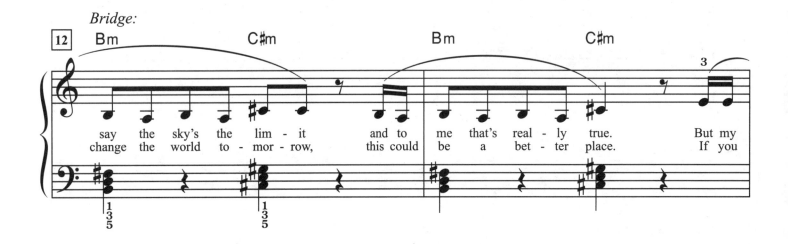

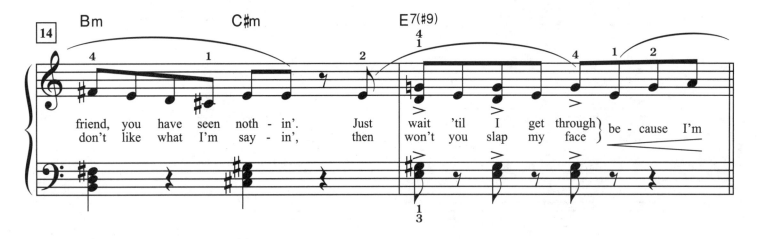

know it. You know I'm bad, I'm bad, you know it, you know. And the

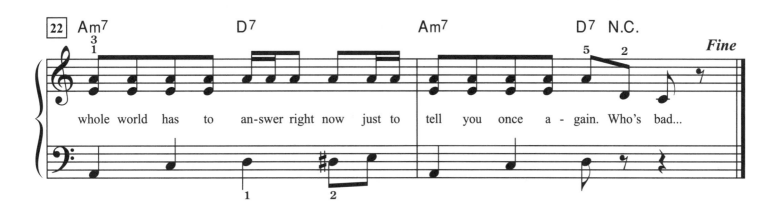

whole world has to an-swer right now just to tell you once a - gain. Who's bad...

3. The

Verse 3:
The word is out, you're doin' wrong.
Gonna lock you up before too long.
Your lyin' eyes gonna tell you right.
So listen up, don't make a fight.
Your talk is cheap, you're not a man.
You're throwin' stones to hide your hands.

BEAT IT

Written and Composed by Michael Jackson
Arranged by Carol Matz

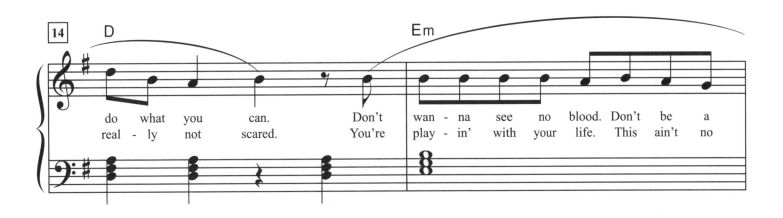

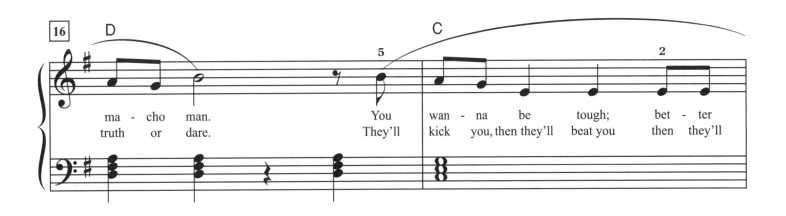

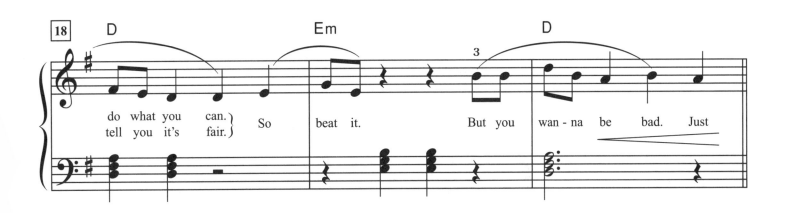

Chorus:

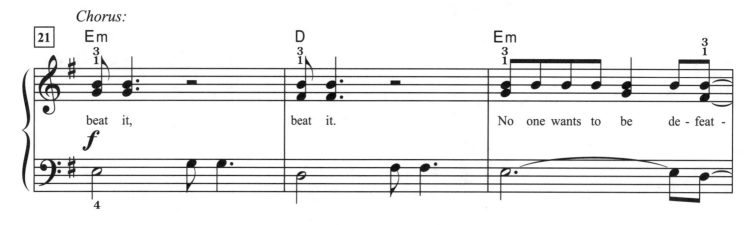

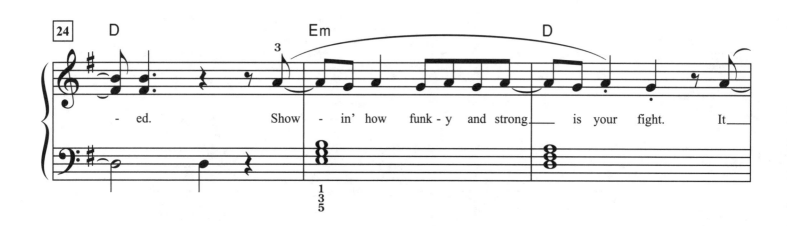

BILLIE JEAN

Written and Composed by Michael Jackson
Arranged by Carol Matz

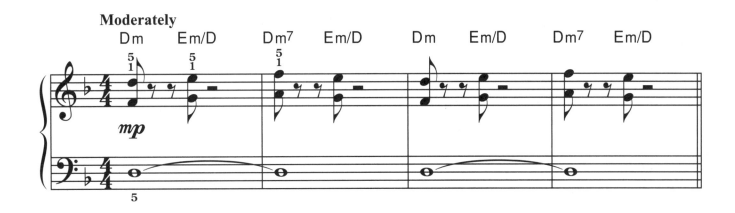

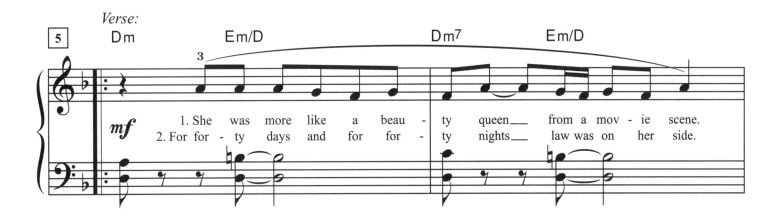

1. She was more like a beau - ty queen___ from a mov - ie scene.
2. For for - ty days and for for - ty nights___ law was on her side.

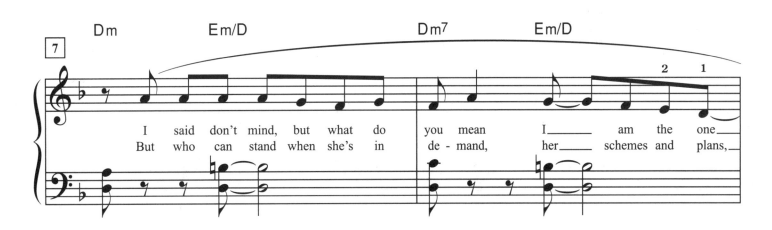

I said don't mind, but what do you mean I___ am the one.
But who can stand when she's in de - mand, her___ schemes and plans,

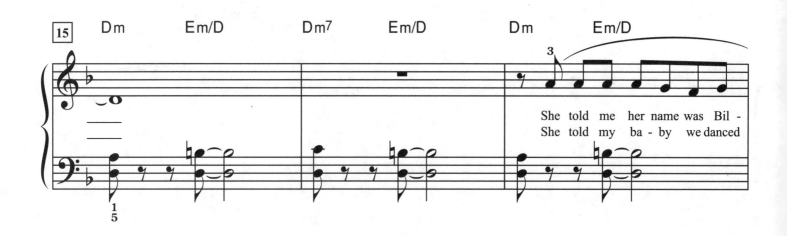

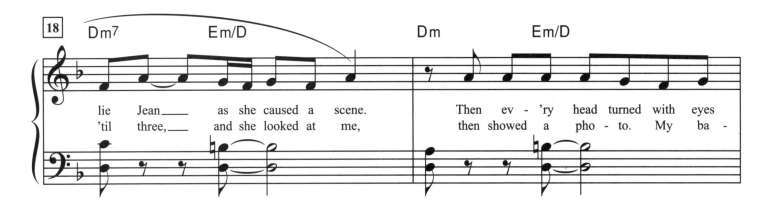

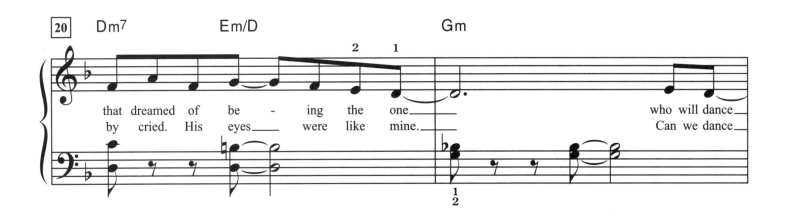

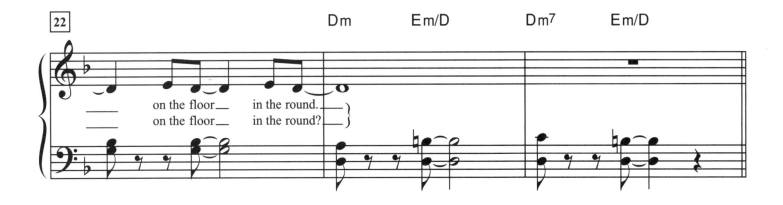

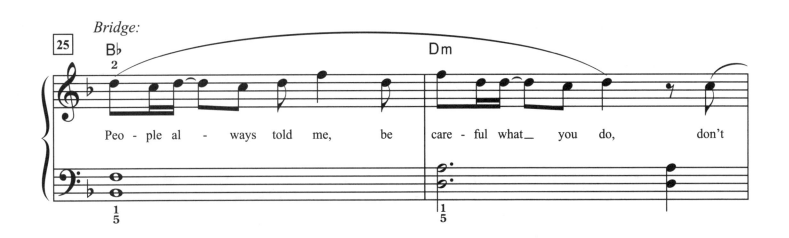

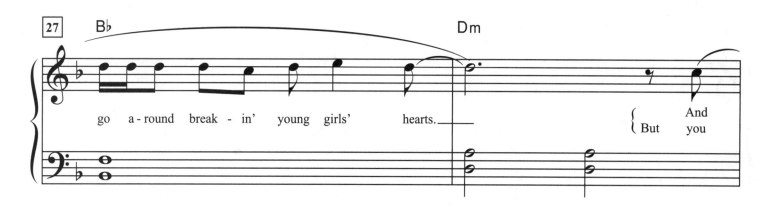

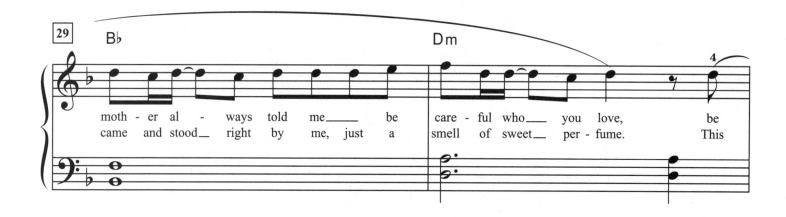

Chorus:

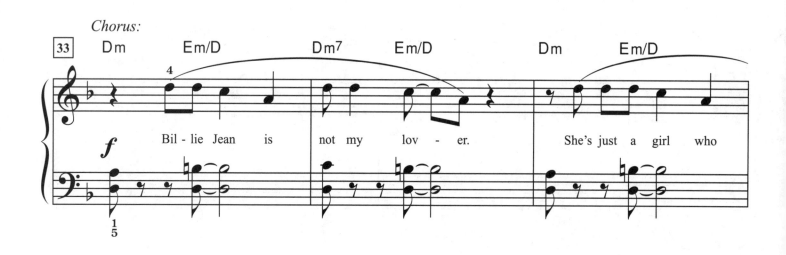

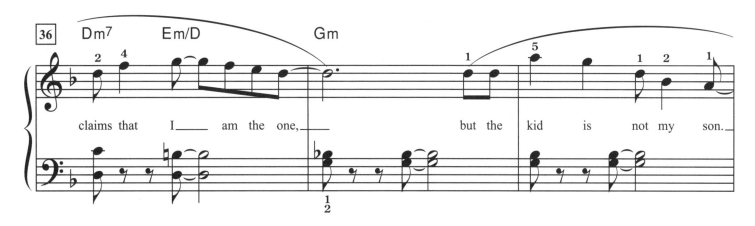

claims that I____ am the one,____ but the kid is not my son.

She says I____ am the one,____ but the

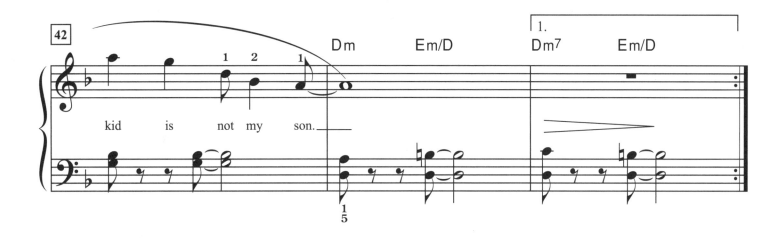

kid is not my son.____

DON'T STOP BELIEVIN'

Words and Music by Jonathan Cain,
Neal Schon and Steve Perry
Arranged by Carol Matz

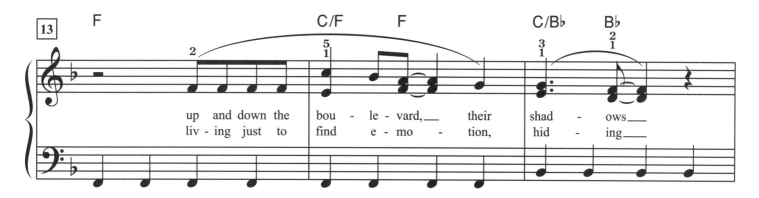

up and down the bou - le - vard,___ their shad - ows___
liv - ing just to find e - mo - tion, hid - ing___

1., 3.

search - ing___ in the night.___

2., 4.

some - where___ in the night.___

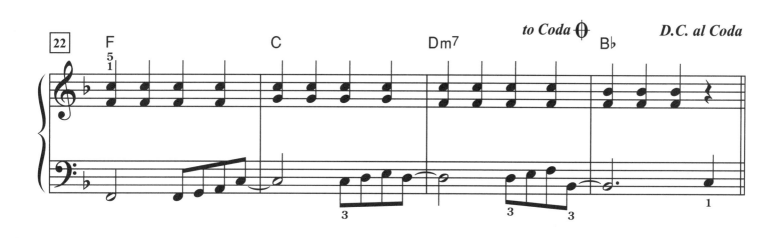

to Coda ⊕   D.C. al Coda

22

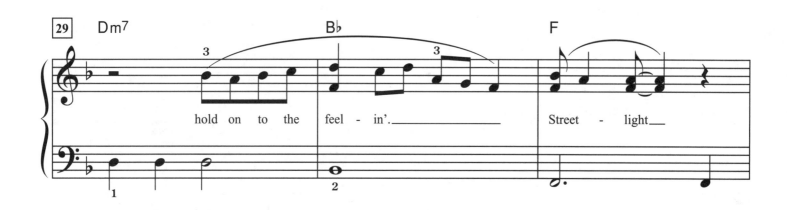

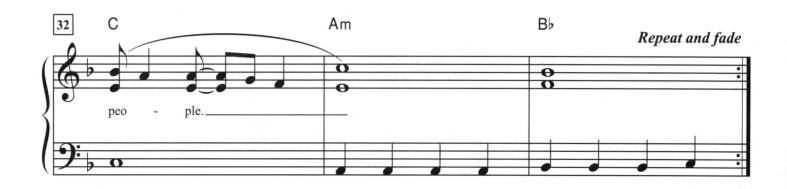

Verse 3:
A singer in a smoky room,
the smell of wine and cheap perfume.
For a smile they can share the night,
it goes on and on and on and on.

Verse 4:
Working hard to get my fill.
Everybody wants a thrill,
payin' anything to roll the dice
just one more time.

Verse 5:
Some will win and some will lose,
some were born to sing the blues.
Oh, the movie never ends,
it goes on and on and on and on.

HOT N COLD

Words and Music by Katy Perry,
Lukasz Gottwald and Max Martin
Arranged by Carol Matz

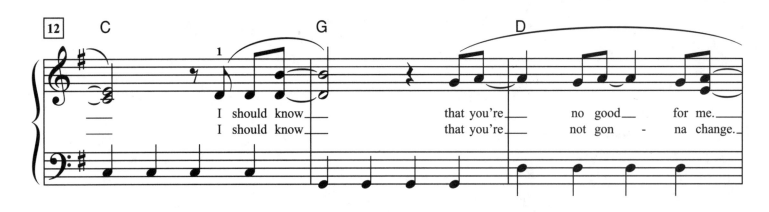

I should know___ that you're___ no good___ for me.___
I should know___ that you're___ not gon - na change.

'Cause you're hot,___ then you're cold. You're yes,

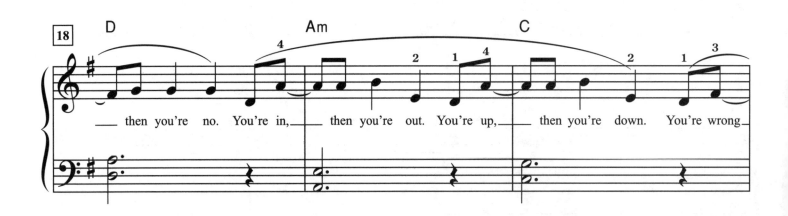

___ then you're no. You're in,___ then you're out. You're up,___ then you're down. You're wrong

___ when it's right. It's black___ and it's white. We fight,___ we break up. We kiss,

26

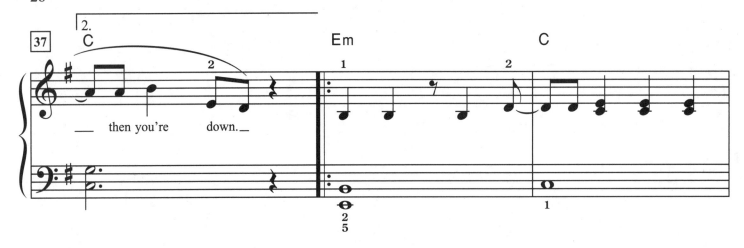

then you're down.

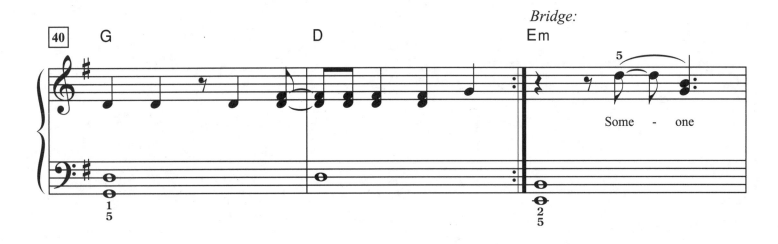

Bridge:

Some - one

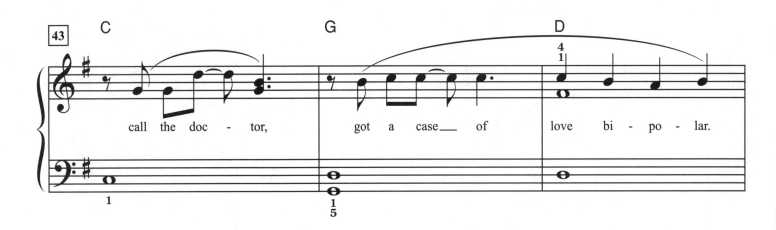

call the doc - tor, got a case___ of love bi - po - lar.

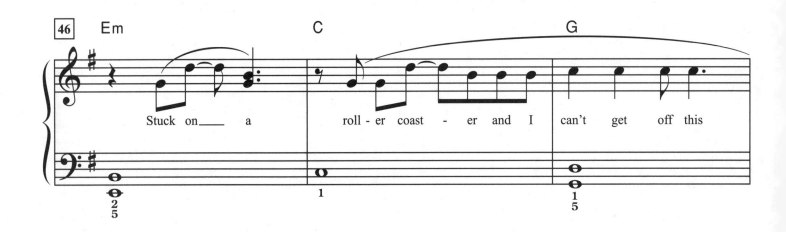

Stuck on___ a roll - er coast - er and I can't get off this

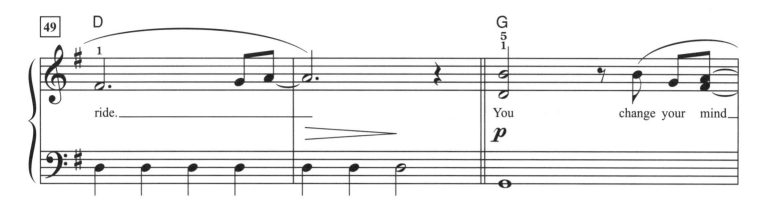

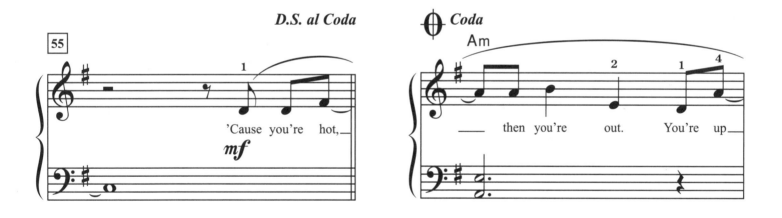

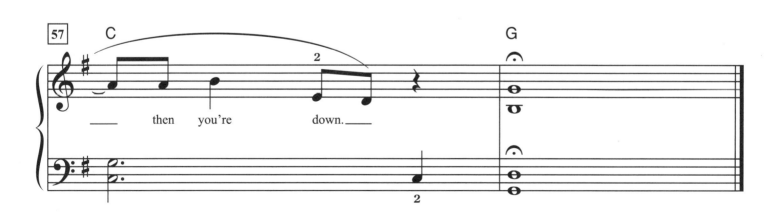

GOTTA BE SOMEBODY

Lyrics by Chad Kroeger
Music by Nickelback
Arranged by Carol Matz

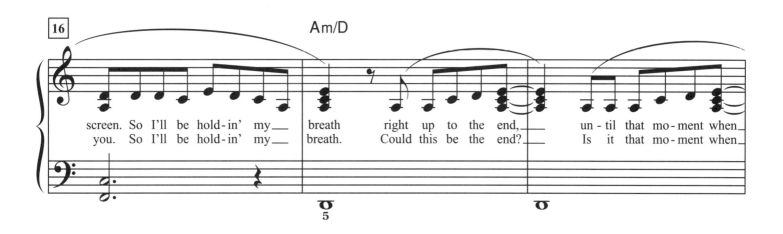

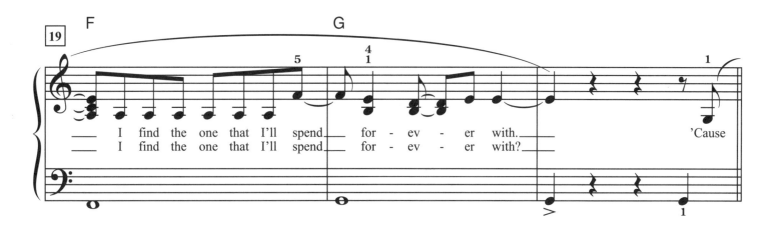

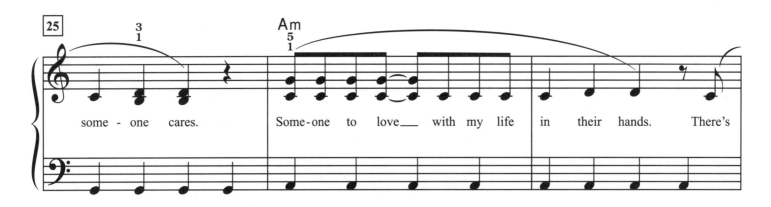

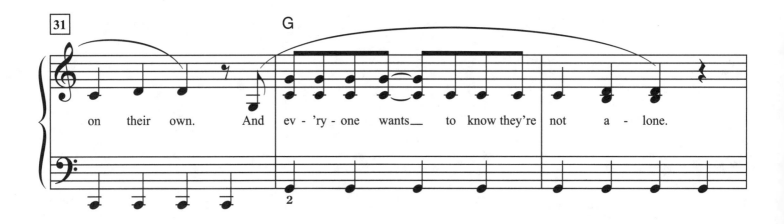

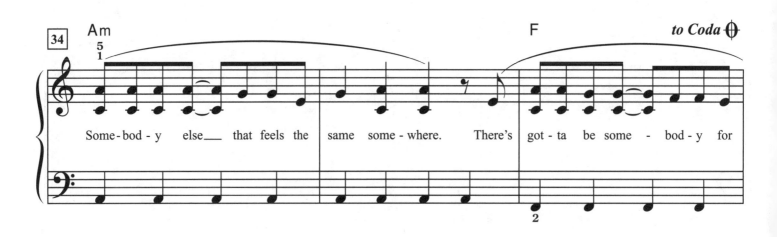

me out there.

me out there. You can't_____ give_____

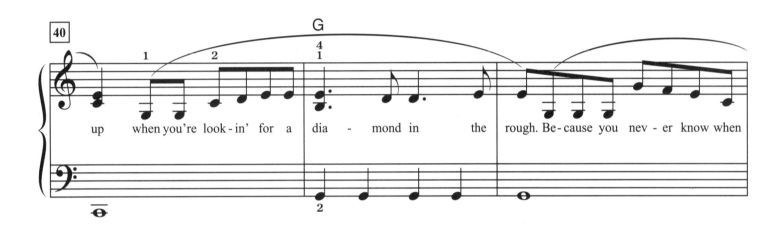

up when you're look-in' for a dia - mond in the rough. Be-cause you nev - er know when

it_____ shows_____ up, make sure you're hold - in on. 'Cause it could be the one,

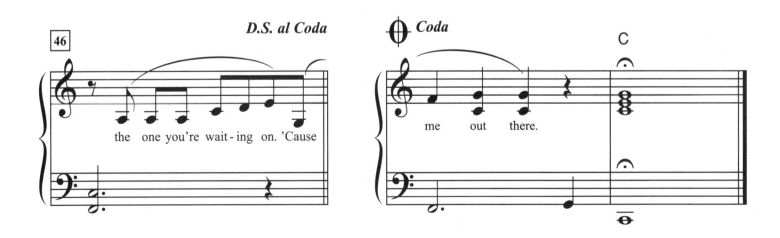

the one you're wait-ing on. 'Cause

me out there.

I KISSED A GIRL

Words and Music by Katy Perry,
Lukasz Gottwald, Max Martin and Cathy Dennis
Arranged by Carol Matz

33

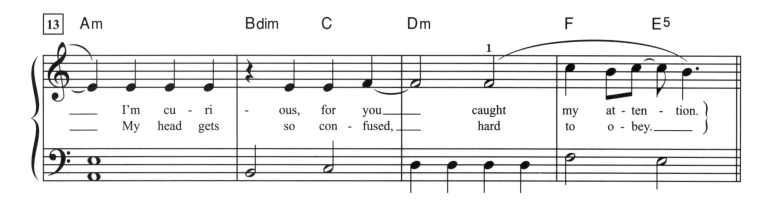

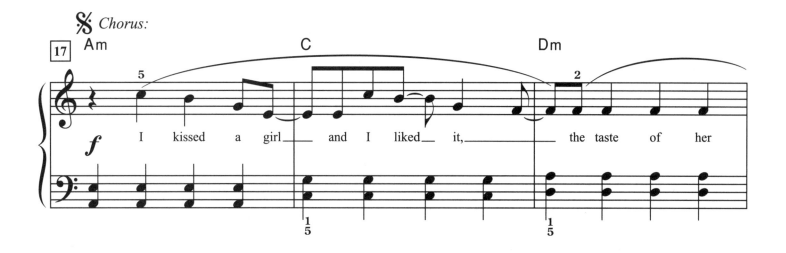

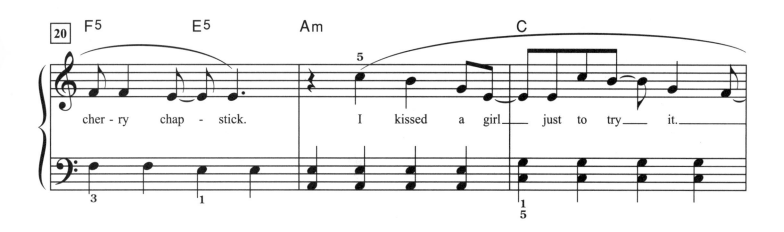

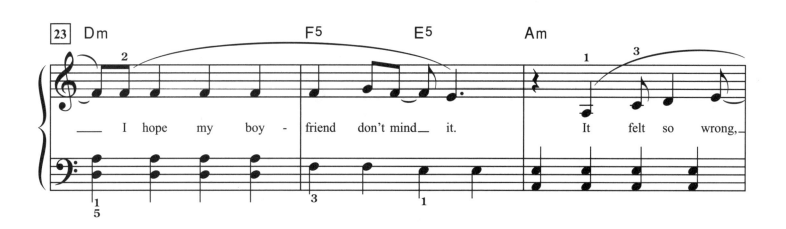

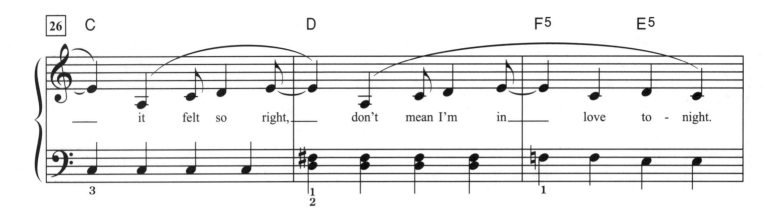

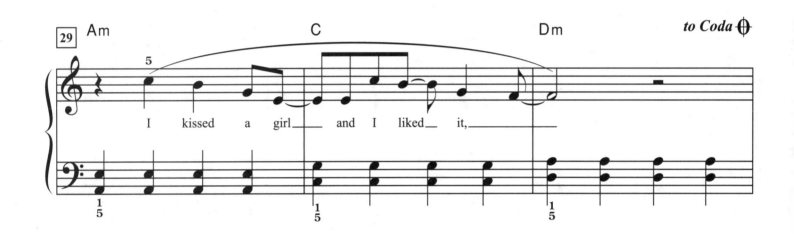

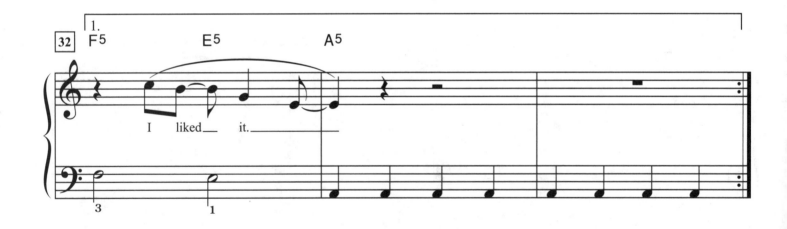

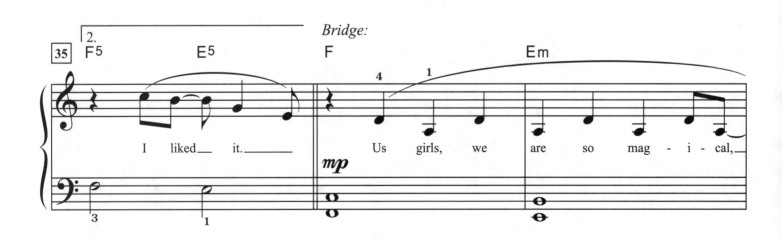

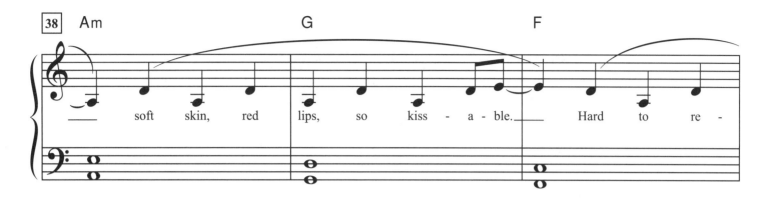

soft skin, red lips, so kiss - a - ble. Hard to re -

sist, so touch - a - ble. Too good___ to de - ny___ it.

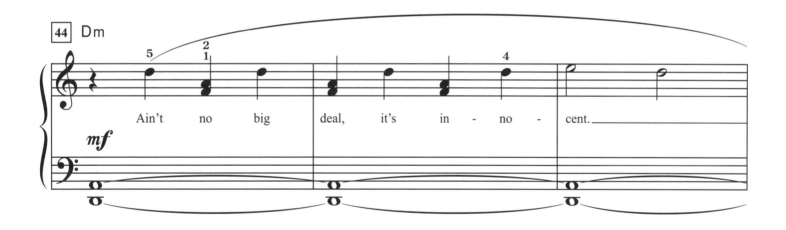

Ain't no big deal, it's in - no - cent.___

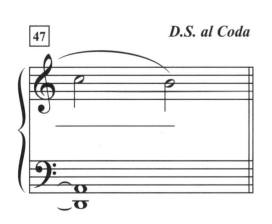

D.S. al Coda

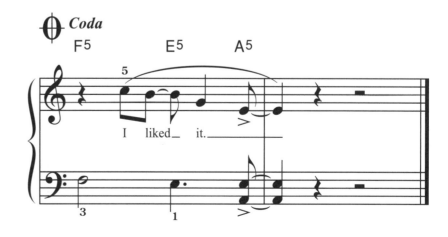

Coda

I liked___ it.___

IN NOCTEM

(from *Harry Potter and the Half-Blood Prince*)

Music by Nicholas Hooper
Lyrics by Steve Kloves
Arranged by Carol Matz

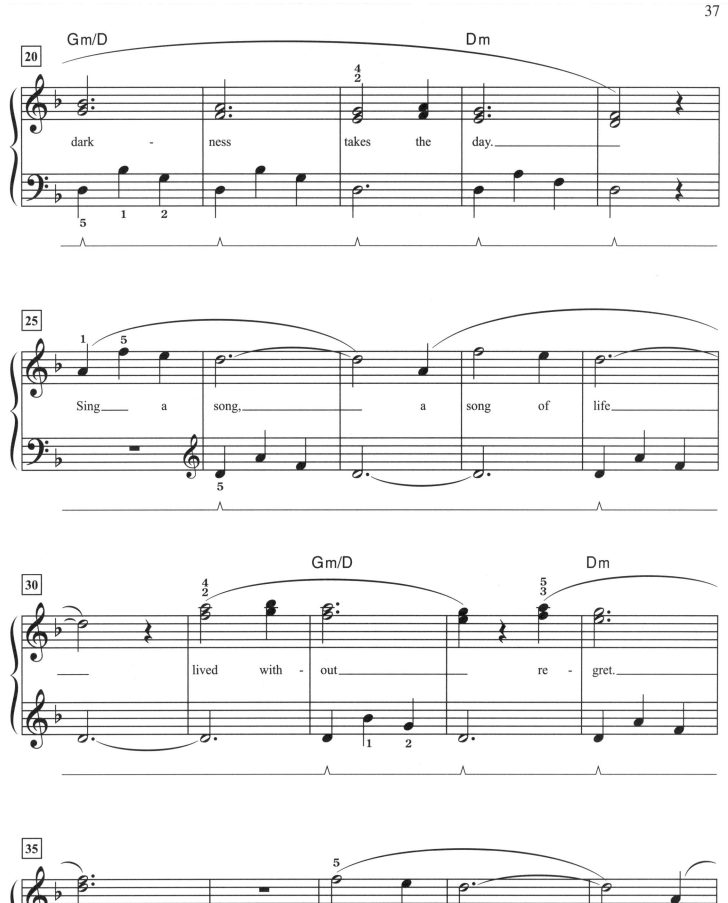

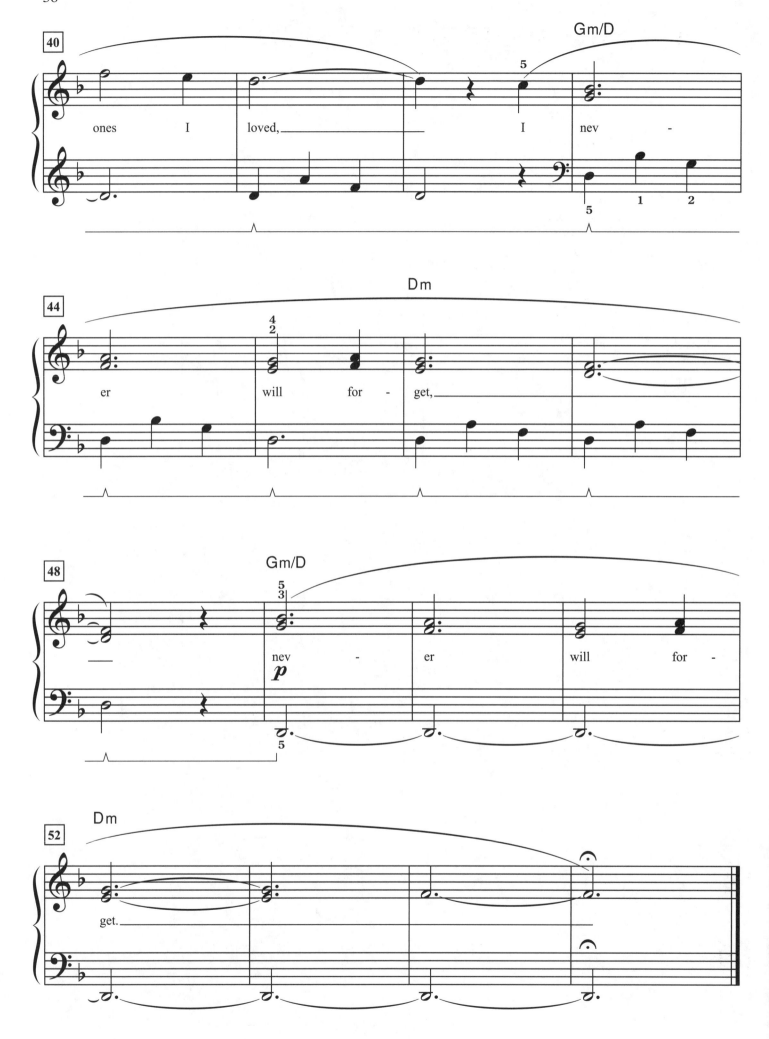

MY LIFE WOULD SUCK WITHOUT YOU

Words and Music by Claude Kelly,
Lukasz Gottwald and Max Martin
Arranged by Carol Matz

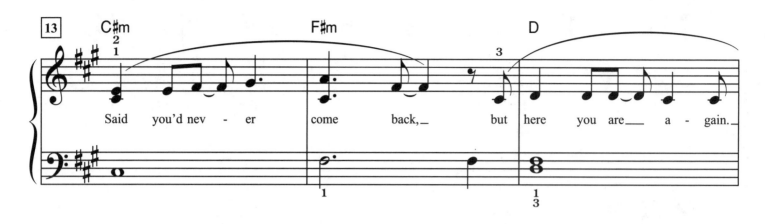

Said you'd nev - er come back, but here you are a - gain.

Chorus:

'Cause we be - long to - geth -

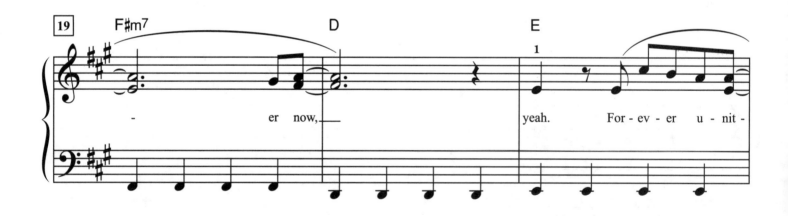

- er now, yeah. For - ev - er u - nit -

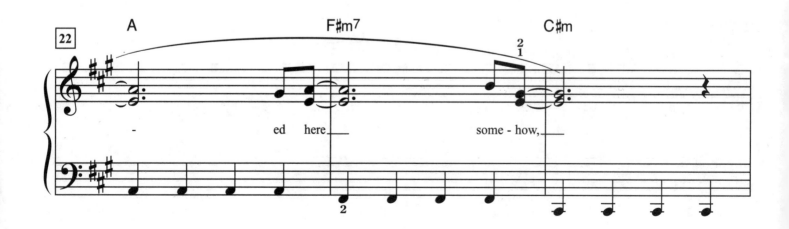

- ed here some - how,

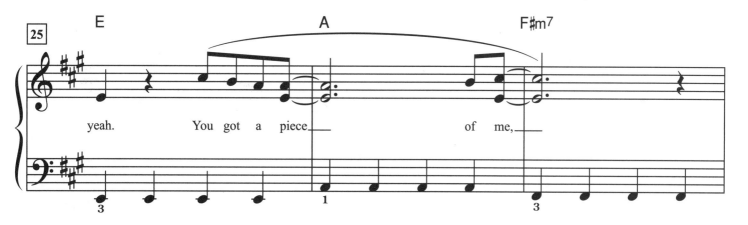

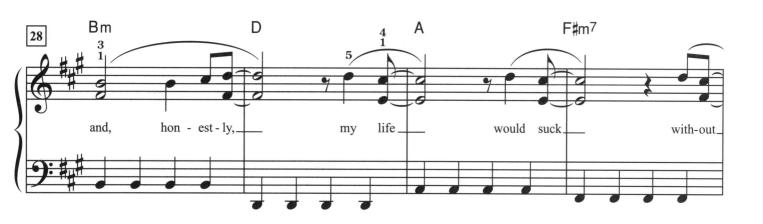

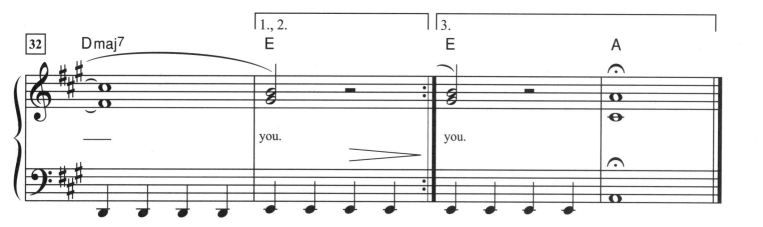

Verse 2:
Baby, I was stupid for telling you goodbye.
Maybe I was wrong for tryin' to pick a fight.
I know that I've got issues, but you're pretty messed up too.
Either way, I found out I'm nothing without you.

Verse 3:
Being with you is so dysfunctional.
I really shouldn't miss you, but I can't let you go, oh, yeah.
(Instrumental)

KNOW YOUR ENEMY

Lyrics by Billie Joe
Music by Green Day
Arranged by Carol Matz

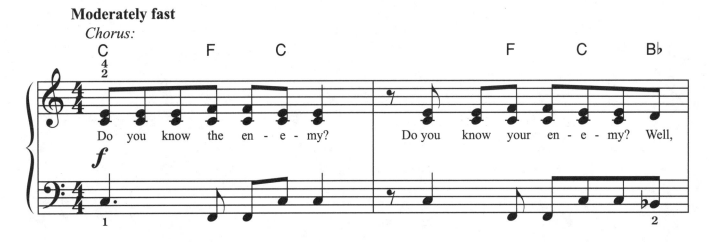

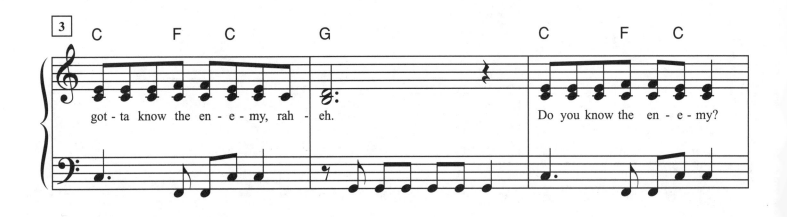

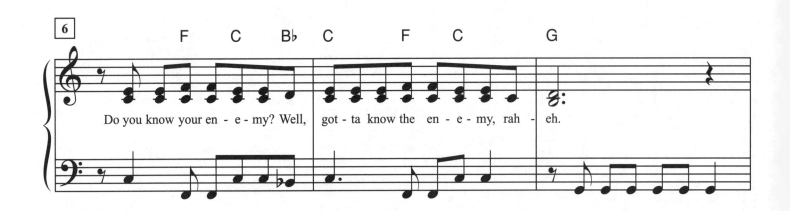

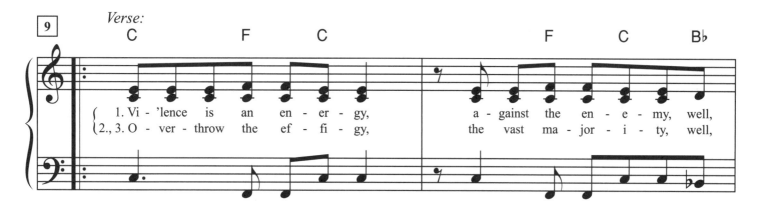

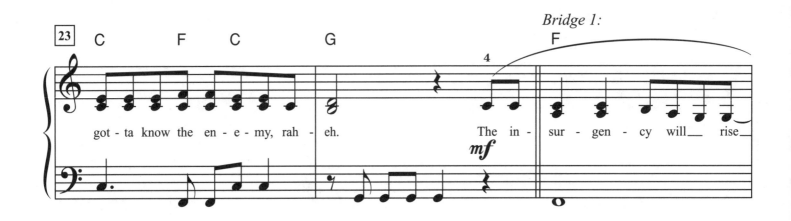

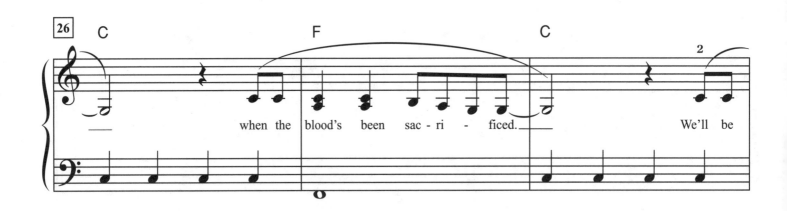

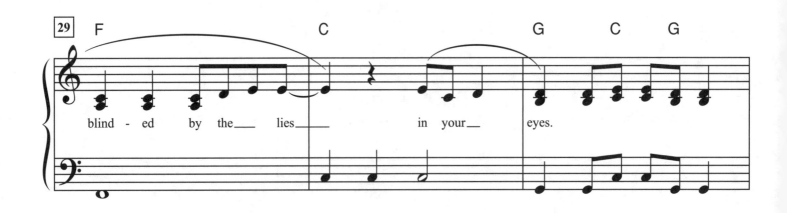

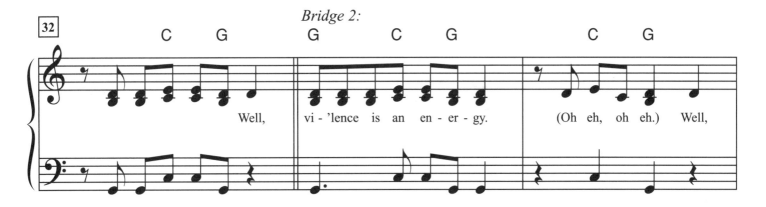

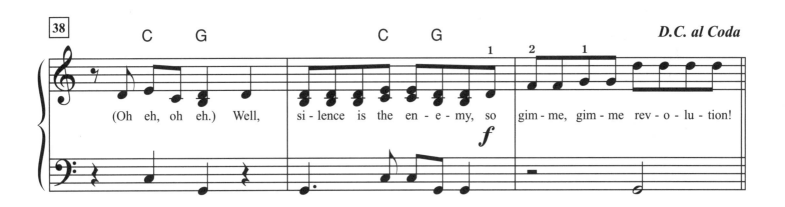

LET IT ROCK

Words and Music by
Kevin Rudolf and Dwayne Carter
Arranged by Carol Matz

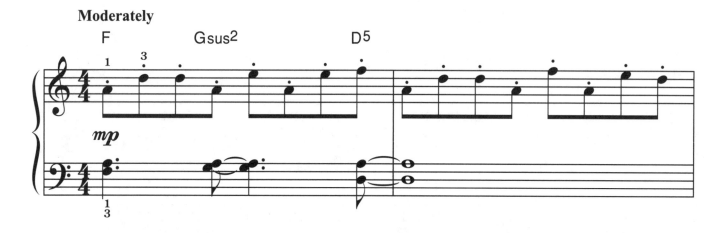

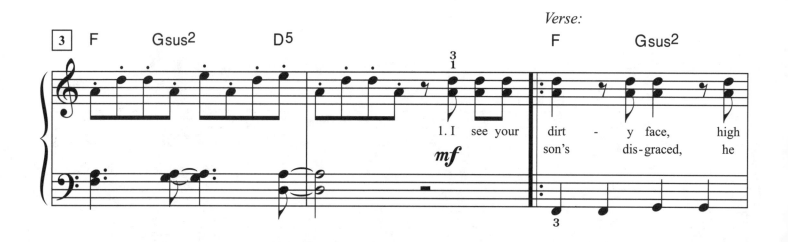

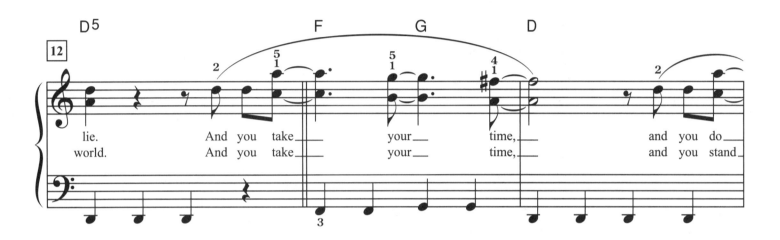

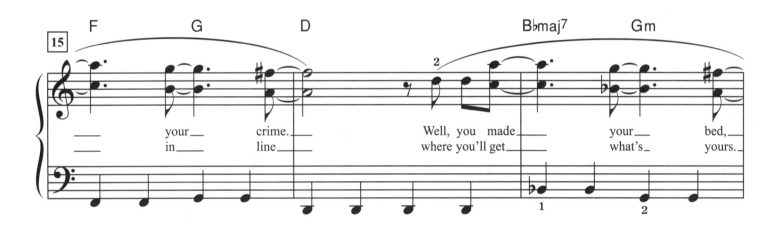

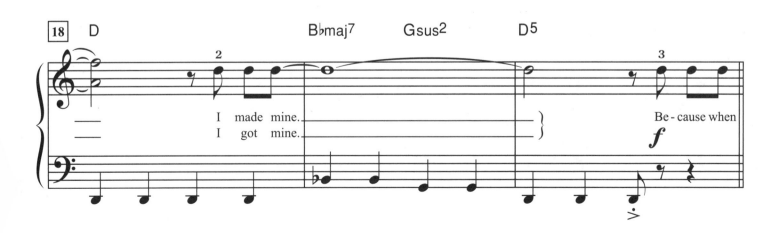

Chorus:

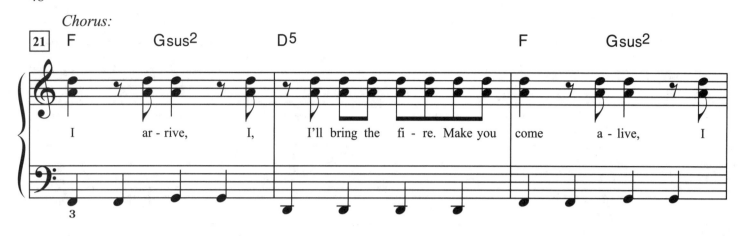

I ar - rive, I, I'll bring the fi - re. Make you come a - live, I

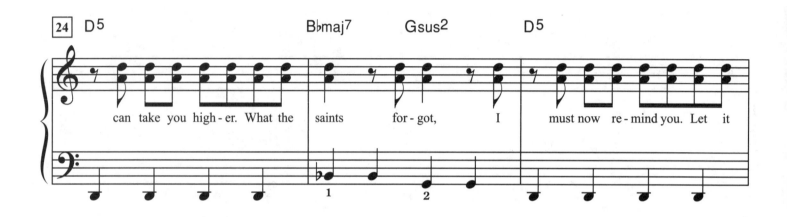

can take you high - er. What the saints for - got, I must now re - mind you. Let it

rock, let it rock, let it rock. 2. Now the rock.

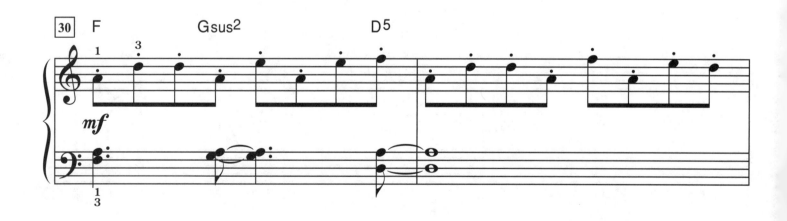

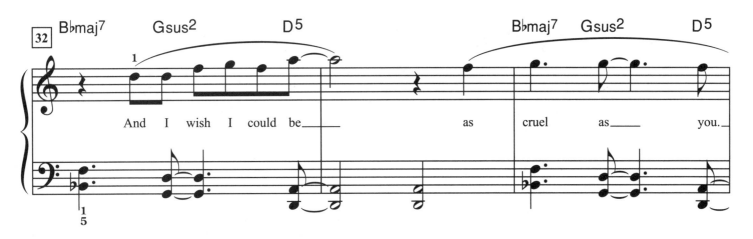

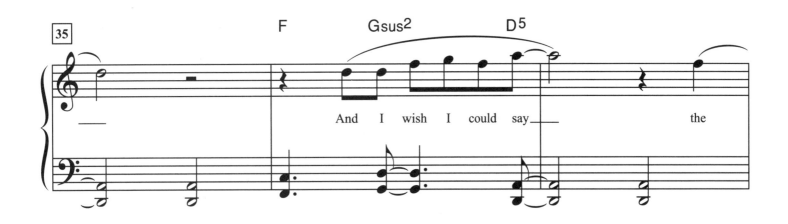

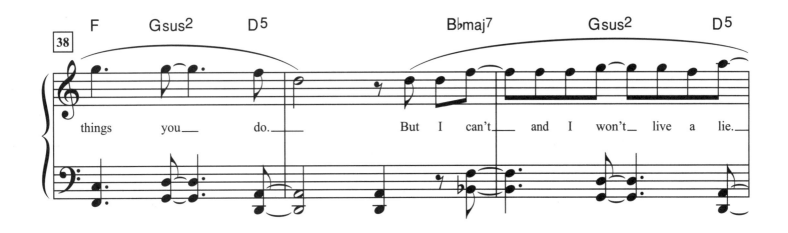

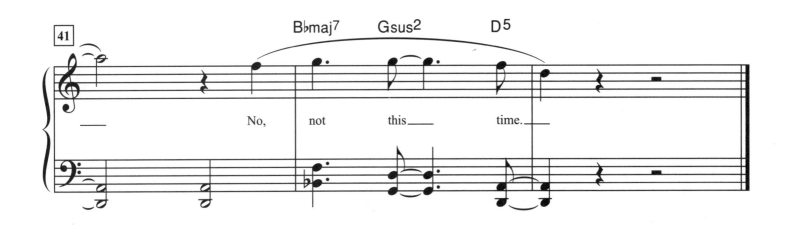

WORKING ON A DREAM

Words and Music by Bruce Springsteen
Arranged by Carol Matz

Chorus:

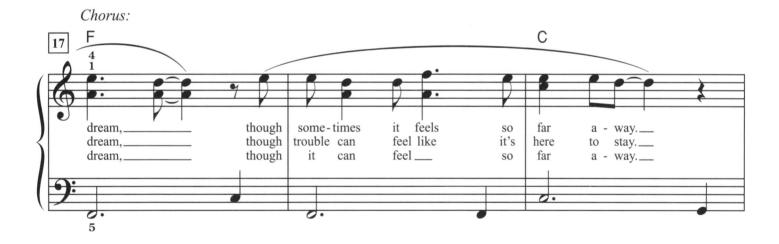

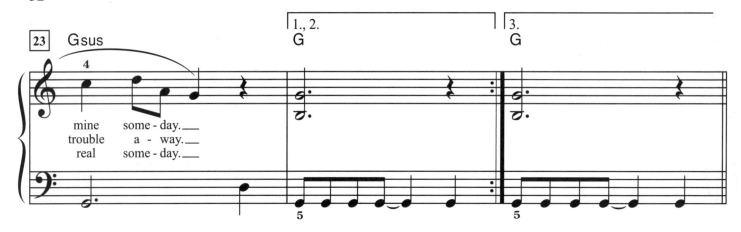

mine some - day.___
trouble a - way.___
real some - day.___

5. Sun - rise come,_ I climb the lad - der. A new day breaks_ and

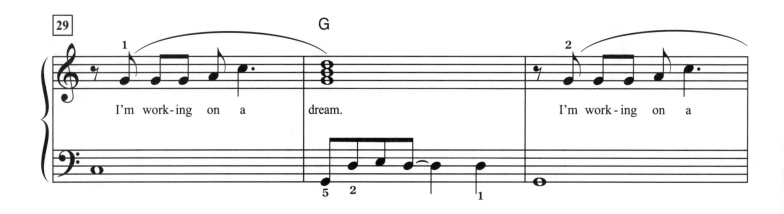

I'm work - ing on a dream. I'm work - ing on a

dream.___ I'm work - ing on a dream.

I'm work-ing on a dream._____ I'm work-ing on a

Chorus:

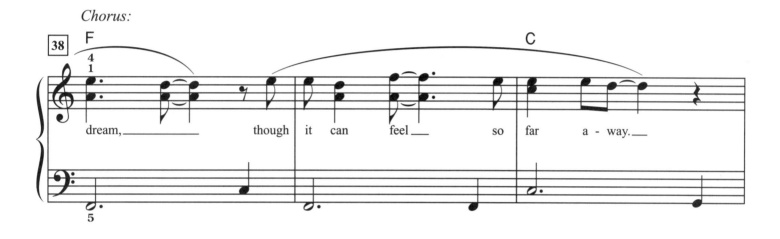

dream,_____ though it can feel___ so far a - way.___

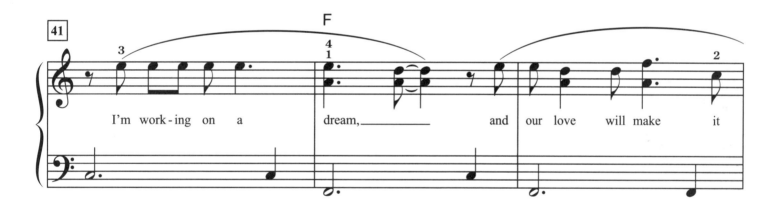

I'm work-ing on a dream,_____ and our love will make it

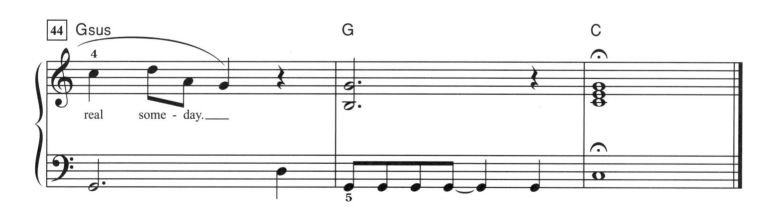

real some - day.___

YOU PULLED ME THROUGH

Words and Music by Diane Warren
Arranged by Carol Matz

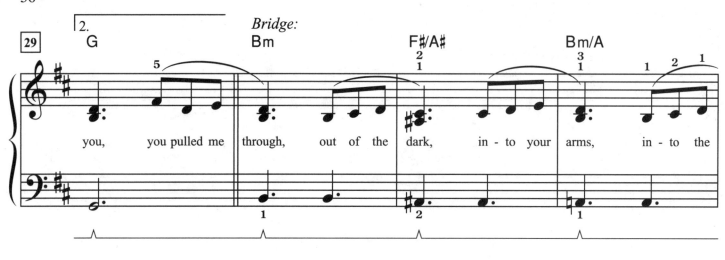

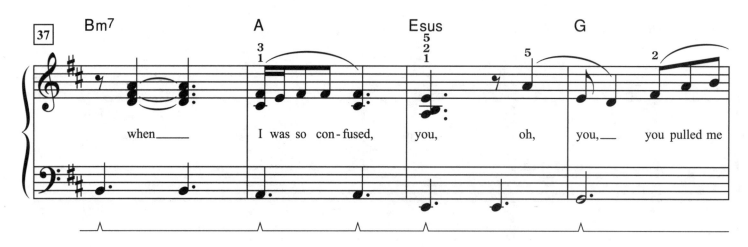

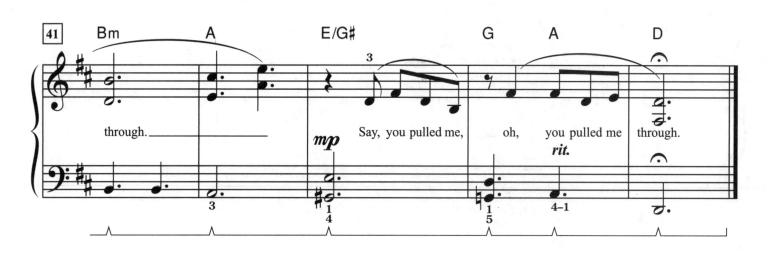